SIOUX WINTER COUNT

A 131-Year Calendar of Events

Roberta Carkeek Cheney

Traditional Interpretation by Kills Two
Illustrations by Ralph Shane

Naturegraph

Library of Congress Cataloging-in-Publication Data
Cheney, Roberta Carkeek.
　　[Big Missouri winter count]
　　A Sioux winter count : 131 years of Dakota history, 1796-1926/
Roberta Carkeek Cheney : traditional interpretation by Kills Two :
Illustrations by Ralph Shane.
　　　　p.　　cm.
　　Originally published: Big Missouri winter count.
　　Includes bibliographical references.
　　ISBN 0-87961-249-5 (alk. paper)
　　1. Dakota calendar. 2. Dakota Indians—History. I. Kills two.
II. Title.
E99.D1C47　1998
978'.004975—dc21
　　　　　　　　　　　　　　　　　　　　　98-21072
　　　　　　　　　　　　　　　　　　　　　CIP

ISBN 0-87961-249-5

Copyright © 1998 by Roberta Carkeek Cheney.

Cover illustration: Kills Two, Brulé Sioux, working on the Big Missouri
Winter Count. Traditional interpretations are also by Kills Two.

Naturegraph Publishers has been publishing books
on natural history, Native Americans,
and outdoor subjects since 1946.
Please write for our free catalog.

Books for a better world

Naturegraph Publishers, Inc.
3543 Indian Creek Road
Happy Camp, CA 96039
(530)493-5353

This book is dedicated to all Indian historians, past and present, who know that "a people without history is like wind on the buffalo grass."

*This is the skin on which are recorded 131 years of Sioux history.
The illustrations reproduced on the following page clarify the
pictographs.*

The Big Missouri Winter Count, 1796 to 1926. Illustrations are rendered from a close observation of each pictograph on the skin.

ACKNOWLEDGMENTS

The author is grateful to Kills Two, a Sioux medicine man, who wrote down the interpretation of the Big Missouri Winter Count, and to the curator of the Sioux Indian Museum in Rapid City, South Dakota, who made the copy available for use. Permission to use these materials was granted by the United States Department of the Interior, Bureau of Indian Arts and Crafts.

Sincere appreciation also goes to the artists. Diane Slickers drew enlargements from a photo of the skin. Ralph Shane made heavy line copies that could be reproduced in print. Shane, whose lifelong interest in Indian history and art led him to make illustrated maps of each Montana reservation, was knowledgeable as well as skillful in creating all other artwork for this book.

CONTENTS

List of Illustrations

INTRODUCTION

Winter counts were the historical calendars of the Sioux.

One part of this great Indian nation lived along the big muddy river, the Missouri, that cut its way across Dakota territory. Their historians kept records of these people on animal skins. The Big Missouri Winter Count is one of the most extensive and best preserved of all these Indian calendars. It is housed in the Sioux Indian Museum in Rapid City, South Dakota. This calendar commemorates 131 years of events in the life of one division along the big Missouri, beginning in 1796 (by the white man's system of reckoning), and ending in 1926. It spans a century of great changes for the western Indians. From the time when only an occasional fur trapper or Jesuit missionary was seen in Dakota land to the time when the tribe's activities were dominated by the white man, an appointed historian drew one pictograph with colored dyes on the buffalo or deer skin at the end of each winter season. As skins deteriorated, the figures were copied onto new hides. The one in the museum is domestic calf skin.

This chosen historian had learned the story of each event from his father and his grandfather, who in most cases had been the historians before him. Now it became his responsibility to help choose an important event each year and to represent it with a drawing on the hide. It was also the historian's duty to interpret the drawings for anyone who had need of the record, and to teach the people in his tribe their history by means of the winter count. The original skin remained in the possession of the historian, but it could be copied if another member of the group wanted one for more ready reference.

The Dakota language was a spoken one, not a written one, and only the simple line drawings were put down to remind tribal members of events and to mark the passage of time. Their history is a matter of great pride to the Dakotas. "A people without history is like wind on the buffalo grass."*

---

* Karol, p. 5

Before the days of the white man's schools, a child learned early which winter count symbol marked the year of his birth. He could then count the number of characters between that symbol and the last one on the record to know how old he was.

The Big Missouri Winter Count reads from left to right, and from top to bottom. Some winter counts began with a figure in the center of the skin and advanced clockwise or counterclockwise in a spiral. Others read in a zig-zag fashion, first left to right, then back from right to left.

Kills Two, a Sioux medicine man, wrote down the interpretation of the Big Missouri Winter Count, and a typed copy of it is kept with the skin itself in the Sioux Indian Museum.

What kinds of things were important enough to be recorded on the winter count? Tabulation of the events represented on the Big Missouri skin shows that fifteen entries signify the deaths of chiefs. Twenty-one record other individuals' deaths. In addition to these, nine references to battles with other tribes involve some deaths too, and five instances of family troubles also led to one or more killings. Some deaths were violent; many were the result of an unknown illness. Smallpox was the scourge of the Indian tribes, and three entries are given over to its ravages. We hear that some people froze to death; others froze their feet so badly that they fell off. One birth is recorded: in 1905, the wife of Leader Charge gave birth to quadruplets.

Severe winter weather caused memorable hardships and claims twelve counts. Food was short and people were hungry, especially if the winter lasted too long. A war bonnet presentation is featured in one drawing, gratitude for plenty of food in two, camps in four, and dances in four.

Eight entries are concerned with the buffalo; several of these with "ghost lodges," held when one member of the tribe was lucky enough to kill a white buffalo, always considered sacred and a sign of good fortune. The entry in 1924 represents a buffalo feast honoring Ralph H. Case, attorney for the Sioux, but this buffalo came from a "preserve" near Valentine, Nebraska. Life for the Indian had changed, and the winter count reflects it wordlessly but poignantly.

White men, other than government officials, are featured in ten pictures. Government men, government issues of supplies, and the reservations dominate the latter part of the Big Missouri Winter Count, and total twenty-four entries. Money, other than government issues, merits one pictograph. That was 1855, Plenty of Money Winter. The band had robbed a guarded stagecoach carrying the payroll for a western fort.

In 1834, the "stars fell," and 1870 was the year the "sun was eclipsed." The Indian picked up the white man's burden as one member of the tribe was killed in World War I. Peace treaties are mentioned twice.

The first time an Indian child went to school dominates a winter, and two later entries record students' running away from St. Francis School and freezing to death.

Horses are drawn many times in connection with hunts. In 1829, *nothing* of consequence happened!

One wonders why the Dakota Nation began, at this particular time, to keep winter counts. The Big Missouri Count began in 1796; Lone Dog's Winter Count, and several copies made from it, began in the winter of 1786-7 and ran through 1876-7, a span of 90 years. Red Horse Owner's Winter Count began in 1786, and has been kept up to date by his granddaughters.

Some have theorized that association with the missionaries and traders gave the Sioux an awareness of dates and awakened in them an interest in keeping track of time. Even if the Indians were thus inspired, they devised their own, and most original, system. But the white man's influence becomes far removed when one studies the winter count of Battiste Good, a peculiar cyclic computation which begins with A.D. 900, and in thirteen figures accounts for the time to A.D. 1700. From 1700 to 1880, a figure marks each year. The entries before 1700 represent legends and mythology. It is possible that from 1700 to around 1775 one family did keep an annual count, the need for a systematic marking of time being generally recognized at that time.

The few references on the Big Missouri Winter Count to geographic locations indicate that the group keeping it lived along that river and ranged from Fort Pierre, South Dakota, to the Platte River in Nebraska. (See the map on page 62.)

The Winter of the Horse Stealing Camp, 1796, falls near the beginning of steady European influx. White man's history during the years just preceding this unique skin record includes the La Verendryes' expedition through Dakota territory in 1742-43, and the presence of French fur trappers and traders who came to live and work among the Indians. The Jesuit missionaries followed soon after. By the Treaty of Paris in 1763, following the French and Indian War, France ceded her possessions west of the Mississippi River to Spain, and the first Spanish trader to appear in the upper Missouri country was Juan Munier, in 1789. Spain decided in 1793 that she must in some way enforce her claims to the upper Missouri. She gave her support to the "Company of Explorers of the Upper Missouri," hoping that these traders could oust the British from the area. Another Spanish expedition, led by James Mackay and John Evans and sent out in the spring of 1795, reached the Mandan camps in September, 1796, and took over the post that had been maintained by British traders. They hoisted the Spanish flag in Dakota land.

Early in that same year, and quite unaware, we presume, of European entanglements, the historian for the Big Missouri Winter Count prepared a fine new buffalo skin and drew upon it his first picture—six hoofmarks, three pointing in one direction and three in the other—to mark the Winter of the Horse Stealing Camp.

It is interesting to watch what was going on in other "camps," including Washington, D.C., during those years between 1796 and 1926, an era which encompasses the struggle between the white man and the red man for this western land. Therefore, for some winters, concurrent historical events have been inserted after the original interpretative words given by Kills Two. Occasionally the interpretation has been amplified by quotations from other winter counts. The words in italics are those of Kills Two.

I

THE BIG MISSOURI WINTER COUNT

1796 *Winter of the Horse Stealing Camp.*

The Dakota hunting pattern was similar to that of other plains Indians. As they acquired horses—often stolen in raids—they became more mobile.

In this year, the "first house" in Dakota was built by Jean Baptiste Trudeau, near present-day Pickstown, South Dakota, called today the "Pawnee House."

The eastern Sioux were driven from Red Lake by the Ojibwa, westward, this same year.

1797 *Death of Chief Bone Bracelet.*

1798 *Death of Chief Buffalo Tail on Head.*

1799 *Very cold winter causing the death of many expectant mothers.*

[Now begins the second row of pictures on the hide, reading left to right.]

1800   Arrival of two friendly white women among the Indians during hostile times. Women were dressed in long black gowns and were so God-like the Indians did not harm them. Afterwards it appeared they might have been Catholic priests, but the pictures indicate the Indians thought they were women.

1801   First good whiteman visited the Indians, a missionary.

1802   Death of great Chief Wounded Hand.

1803   Crows and Sioux met while both were hunting buffalo. Being enemies, a fight ensued. Blinding snowstorm arose suddenly, both parties had to camp. After the storm they discovered they were camped close together and a second fight ensued.

The year of the Louisiana Purchase, by which the United States claimed all the land from the Mississippi to the Rockies, and from the Gulf of Mexico to Canada.

1804 A Frenchman came among the Indians. Was known as "Little Beaver." Made his home on an island in the Missouri River.

Presumably this was Loisel, a member of the firm of Glamorgan, Loisel and Co., organized in 1789 as a successor to the original Missouri Company. "In 1800 Loisel received permission to form a trading establishment on the Upper Missouri. When his way up the river was blocked by the Dakota, he built a fortified post on Decar Island about 35 miles below Ft. Pierre. Fort *aux Cedres* remained a stopping place for traders and explorers until its destruction by fire about 1810."*

1805 An Omaha Indian, enemy of the Sioux, ventured into Sioux camp and was killed.

On April 7, 1805, Lewis and Clark left Fort Mandan, where they had camped for the winter, and began their arduous trip west. They had had several encounters with the Teton Dakota, often called "the pirates of the Missouri." Only the firm actions of Captain Clark, taken at the risk of hostility and bloodshed, caused the Dakota to give up their apparent plan to prevent the expedition from advancing farther up the river.

On September 23, the eastern Sioux in the Minnesota area made their first treaty with the U. S. They gave a tract of land for an undecided amount, while liquor was generously distributed. In 1808, the treaty was ratified, but never proclaimed.

---

* Schell, p. 36

[Third Row]

*1806   Delegation of Indians and wives started
to Washington to see the "Great Father." Em-
barked in rawhide boats on Missouri River.
Did not know where they left the Missouri for
Washington, but were gone so long the Indians
thought them all lost. A few finally came back.*

Note the lines indicating "many" and the hat
indicating a whiteman that is held up by one of
the lines or sticks. This must be a reference to
the Mandan chief She-he-ke (Big White) who
finally agreed to accompany Lewis and Clark
back to St. Louis and Washington, D.C.,
provided his wife and children, and another
woman and her children, could go too. They
left Dakota territory on August 17, 1806.
"Sergeant Pryor was the leader of the party
which unsuccessfully attempted to return
Chief She-he-ke to his village in 1807. She-
he-ke eventually got home."*

In this year Congress passed an act establishing trading posts west of the Mississippi, and
strictly controlling Indian trade.

*1807   Crow Indian sneaked into Sioux camp
and was killed.*

The Crows, who were later to befriend the
white man and act as his scouts, were tradi-
tionally a peaceful tribe, often harassed by
the more war-like Dakota.

*1808   Indians expressed gratitude to Provi-
dence in profuse manner by putting many red
flags on hills, rocks, and other conspicuous
places.*

At the headwaters of the Missouri in what was
later to become Montana, John Colter, recent-

---

* Salisbury, p. 222

ly returned from exploring the Yellowstone thermal area, took John Potts and went to Three Forks, hoping to establish a trading post there. Blackfoot Indians captured them, killed Potts, and Colter barely escaped.

1809   Feed so scarce Indians had to feed horses on bark of trees which they cut down. Man named "Kettle" and his son killed by falling trees.

1810   Frenchman, "Little Beaver," mentioned in 1804, established his home on an island. House burned down.

This would seem to verify the assumption that "Little Beaver" was Loisel.

1811   The Sioux (Dakota) stole a buckskin horse from the Crow Indians. Its mane and tail were decorated with eagle feathers. Later it became a famous racehorse among the Sioux.

On July 17, 1811, Wilson Price Hunt, a partner of John Jacob Astor, left the Arikara villages and struck out for the Black Hills, and thence to the Big Horn Mountains. "This first overland passage westward across the present state of South Dakota was made by a party of 60 persons, with 118 horses—76 of them loaded with merchandise and equipment."*

---

* Schell, p. 47

*1812   The snow was so deep the men could not
hunt buffalo. Instead they trapped eagles by
decoying them with bait to holes where the
hunters were hidden.*

The War of 1812 produced a crisis for the
American fur trader and gave British traders
an opportunity to draw the Dakota and other
tribes to their side. The Santee Dakota were
allied with the British and drew in other
western tribes.

*1813   Friendly whiteman peddled his goods.
The marks indicate those made by the trader
in keeping his accounts.*

*1814   A Pawnee carrying the first gun the
Sioux had seen was killed.*

Presumably, the guns were given to the Indians during and after the War of 1812, and
though this Indian historian and his Dakota
group had not seen a gun, other Dakota no
doubt had them.

Manuel Lisa was sent in this year, by the American government, to establish trading posts.

*1815   An enemy who came into camp was
killed by Red Son-in-Law with a tomahawk.*

Before this time, small skins were supplied to
the traders. In this year, the commercial
potential of the buffalo was recognized and
started a demand for their skins. The Teton
Dakota developed a prosperous trade with the
white men and became less hostile.

Sioux and Ojibwa chiefs met for their first
peace council.

On July 19, separate bands signed the first of several treaties with the U. S., one of which defined the Sioux-Ojibwa boundary.

1816   Camped south of the Niobrara River, the Sioux hunted and roped wild horses.

[Fourth Row]

1817   Death of Chief Band Hand.

1818   A sudden blizzard froze ducks and geese in flight. The ground and even tipis were covered with dead birds.

In a Congressional act on April 16, the President and Senate were given sole authority to appoint Indian agents and traders.

1819   The winter many Sioux were killed by smallpox.

On March 3, a Congressional act and appropriation for Indian education was passed. This served as the legal basis for most of the educational work carried out by the U. S. government.

Secretary of War, John C. Calhoun, drew up plans for military posts to protect the fur traders in Indian country. Fort Atkinson, in what is now Nebraska, was established that year.

1820   A whiteman built his house on Sioux lands without permission.

1821   The Sioux dragged logs by horses to build a house for a whiteman named Joseph, the grandfather of David Gallineaux.

1822   Joseph, the whiteman, brought much whiskey among the Sioux. He traded a jugful for a mule.

1823   Slicer had his feet and legs frozen so badly they came off.

Also in 1823, Prince Paul of Wurttemberg came to the United States and went up the Missouri River. Later he traveled overland through the Dakota country to a fur post operated by Joshua Pilcher on the Missouri, above the present town of Chamberlain, South Dakota.

1824   The winter was so severe that the Sioux camped near a fine field of corn raised by a whiteman. He gave them corn to eat.

Extremely cold weather, lack of food, and the part played by the white man in the Indians' lives are factors that come to be mentioned more and more often in the winter count.

In 1824, Jedediah Smith and his group left the

Wind River valley where they had wintered with the Crow Indians. "Suffering terribly from icy blizzards, thirst, and hunger, they rediscovered South Pass that. . .the Astorians had first used in 1812."*

In this year, the Secretary of War, John C. Calhoun, created the Bureau of Indian Affairs under his Department. Calhoun advocated destruction of tribes and a "guardianship" status for Indians.

1825   *Two hungry half-breed youths, finding a dead buffalo on the prairie, ate some of the meat and died. Yellow Eyes, a whiteman, was father of one of the boys.*

On June 22, the Teton, Yankton and Yanktonais bands signed a U. S. treaty for friendship between tribes, for boundaries and regulations.

July 16, the Hunkpapa band signed a treaty acknowledging U. S. supremacy, and regulating trade.

August 19, a U. S. treaty was signed by the eastern Sioux for permanent peace with the Sac, Fox, Menominee, Iowa, and Winnebago, covering the mining areas of Minnesota and Wisconsin.

1826   *Many Sioux, camped along the Missouri River, were drowned in a spring flash flood.*

---

* Lavender, p. 82

1827   The countryside was so icy the hunters could not use horses, so went on foot. When game was killed, it was tied in the hide and dragged home.

In 1827, twenty-five trappers under the leadership of Sylvester Pratte left St. Louis on a fur trading expedition. Pratte died in Colorado and the others went on to the "Green River Valley in Wyoming, but there they were immobilized by one of the most merciless winters on record."*

1828   A young woman, abused by her husband, fled to her father, Walking Crow. Her husband pursued her to her father's tipi, attacked the father, and returned to his own tipi. Walking Crow followed the husband and shot him to death.

1829   The winter nothing of consequence happened.

In this year, Andrew "Stonewall" Jackson took office and made official the policy of Indian removal westward, which was unchanged until Grant's inauguration in 1869.

1830   Hair Brushed Back from Forehead obtained a sacred white buffalo hide and consecrated it in the name of his deceased son by keeping a "Ghost Lodge," a sign of good will for all men.

Jim Bridger and others established the Rocky Mountain Fur Company. And in this year, the Indian Removal Act passed through Congress, authorizing the removal of all Indians to west of the Mississippi River, depending on their consent.

---

* Lavender, p. 87

On July 15th of this year, a few eastern Sioux, as well as Sac and Fox, signed a treaty giving the U. S. title to land in Minnesota, Missouri, and Iowa, including timber, mining, and grazing rights.

[Fifth Row]

1831   Four white buffaloes were killed, the largest number in history. Swift Bear owned the only horse fast enough to capture them.

In *Cherokee Nation v. Georgia*, the U. S. Supreme Court claimed that Indians have "an unquestionable. . .right to the lands which they occupy, until that right shall be extinguished by a voluntary cession to our government. . . ."

1832   An enemy tribe made friends with the Sioux and they camped together during the winter.

Congress created the office of U. S. Commissioner of Indian Affairs in the Department of War, and made an appropriation for smallpox vaccinations for Indians.

The U. S. Supreme Court in *Worcester v. Georgia* ruled that the Cherokee and other Indian nations were "distinct, independent, political communities, retaining their political rights."

1833   The winter many Omahas were killed. The Omahas wore high-topped moccasins.

Maximilian, Prince of Wied (in Germany), an exploring naturalist, visited and studied the Missouri River valley. George Catlin began his great career of sketching and portrait painting among the western Indians in 1832. The

Big Missouri Winter Count keeper seemed quite unaware of these foreign visitors, or else he thought them of little importance.

The record of White Cow Killer calls this "One-Horn's leg-broken-winter." Catlin painted this chief in 1832 and described him as Head Chief of all the Dakota. He was later gored to death by a buffalo bull.

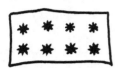

1834   The winter the stars fell.

Every winter count that has been studied records this great meteoric shower as did the white man's records for November 12, 1833. "Winter" includes parts of two calendar years: thus the November 1833 incident was reported by the Big Missouri historian at the end of that winter, 1834. Other winter counts called it "Storm of stars winter," and "Plenty-stars winter," representing it as six four-pointed stars over a crescent moon or a shower of stars around the moon.

By this year, sixty schools had been established among various tribes through the efforts of six religious organizations and Indians themselves. Nearly 2,000 children were presently enrolled under 137 teachers.

Congress established the U. S. Department of Indian Affairs in 1834, in an effort at reorganization.

In the Indian Trade and Intercourse Act, which strengthened the government's control on intruders, Indian territory was defined as "all that part of the United States west of the Mississippi, and not within the states of Missouri and Louisiana, or the territory of Arkansas, and, also, that part of the United States east of the Mississippi River, and not within any state to which the Indian title has not been extinguished."

1835   *A Cheyenne who married a Sioux girl during peace between the tribes, deserted her when war broke out. He was then thought to have joined other Cheyennes in killing a Sioux boy during a raid upon a camp. After the war, when the Cheyenne returned to his wife, he was killed with a tomahawk by a Sioux.*

1836   *The Sioux were defeated in battle, but only the two leaders, who held off the enemy while the main body escaped, were killed.*

Other winter counts list this as the year that a Two Kettle, named The Breast, died.

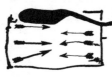

1837   *The Pawnees and the Sioux fought across the frozen Platte River with arrows. Those daring enough to go on the ice were killed.*

On September 29, in Washington, the eastern Sioux ceded all their land east of the Mississippi for annuities and goods.

1838   *A Sioux of the Broken Bow Camp stole the wife of a Sioux from another camp. This created so much feeling that the man from Broken Bow was killed.*

1839   *A white trader conducted his store in a tipi.*

1840   The winter the Sioux camped on a hill. Usually they placed their villages along protected streams.

This year marked the approximate end of fighting with the Ojibwa over present-day North Dakota.

Also in this year, a high plains alliance was established from the Black Hills to Texas, when the Cheyenne and Arapaho made peace with the Sioux, Kiowa, Kiowa Apache, and Comanche. The alliance, formed at a great council on the Arkansas River, was never broken.

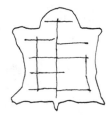

1841   Death of the Great Medicine Man, famous because he could change common substances into important necessities like tobacco, powder, lead and sugar, and noted because he wore a gaily painted robe.

1842   Death of Yellow Eyes, the whiteman who lost his son in 1825.

1843   Many dead buffalo calves were discovered this spring, though whether they were frozen or killed by disease could not be determined.

[Sixth Row]

1844   Cheyennes brought great herds of horses to exchange for sacred Cheyenne Arrow. By the Arrow the Cheyennes could predict the success or failure of war. If blood were found on it, the battle was abandoned; if clean, the battle would be won. The Pawnees had captured the Arrow and the Sioux had recaptured it for the Cheyennes.

During this and the following year, the House passed several bills to protect immigrants and traders with new forts along the westward trails.

1845   Many Pawnees were killed and captured. The Pawnees had made a great buffalo kill and those unable to take part in the hunt were surprised by the Sioux as they were cleaning up the scraps.

1846   The Without Bows, a northern division of the Sioux who formerly remained aloof, camped with the other Sioux this winter.

Fifteen thousand Mormons were driven out of Nauvoo, Illinois. In their long trek toward Utah they were to encounter many hostile Indians and even more hostile whites.

1847   Tall Joe, a whiteman, and his Sioux wife lost a grown son by drowning.

1848   Yellow Spider obtained a sacred white buffalo hide and kept a "Ghost Lodge."

By the treaty of Guadalupe Hidalgo with Mexico, the United States laid claim to all of the western part of the continent between Mexico and Canada.

1849   The winter was so cold that many people in the Bone Camp had frozen feet.

Gold was discovered in California, and prospectors began to cross Indian lands in ever increasing numbers. The Plains Wars began in earnest.

The Bureau of Indian Affairs was transferred from the War Department to the Interior Department, which was concerned with the "liquidation" of the American national estate. Indian lands, along with timber and mineral rights were turned over to individuals and corporations in this process. There had been an unsuccessful effort in government to create a new department to deal only with Indian affairs.

1850   The "One Offering" winter in which the director of ceremonies offered only one red banner to Providence instead of seven. For this error in failing to honor the Four Directions, Heaven, Earth, and All Between, he was ostracized.

Jim Bridger was guiding a party of surveyors who sought a pass over the Continental Divide. They discovered what was to be called Bridger Pass, and would later point the way for wagon roads, stagecoaches, and possibly railroads. The Big Missouri historian could not have foreseen this fateful development, though he did look in all Four Directions, to the Heavens, to the Earth, and to All Between.

1851   The second time many Sioux were killed by smallpox.

"Under the 'treaty of Traverse des Sioux,' negotiated in July 1851, the Santee Sioux (Dakota) had ceded all the lands east of the Big Sioux River except for a reservation area."*

1852   The Big Issue winter when along the Platte River the Government gave a great supply of food and clothing to Arapahoes, Cheyennes, Crows, Sioux and others.

One of the largest gatherings ever of prairie tribes, this was the first treaty of Fort Laramie, granting the U. S. government the right to build and protect forts along the Oregon Trail in return for annuities. Although the treaty was never ratified, it designed the pattern for the next forty years.

1853   The winter was so cold and snowy and feed so scarce that nearly all the horses died. Men hunted on foot and packed the burdens.

1854   Death of Chief Banded Knee.

The first serious Sioux fighting against U. S. troops in what was to become Nebraska occurred during this year.

---

* Schell, p. 72

1855 *Plenty of Money Winter. The Sioux robbed a guarded stagecoach carrying the payroll for a western fort and took all the money. Spotted Tail, the leader, was later arrested and imprisoned.*

"General W. S. Harney was given command of a campaign against the western Sioux. His defeat of a group of Brulés led by Chief Little Thunder terrified all Teton bands, and several years of relative peace followed."*

1856 *War Bonnet Winter. This year war bonnets were given to the bravest warriors who were charged with leading future battles.*

[Seventh Row]

1857 *Year of Great Plenty. Camped near what is now Rosebud, the Sioux killed such quantities of buffalo that great stores were dried for future use.*

In May 1857, representatives of the Dubuque (Iowa) Company successfully occupied a town site along the Big Sioux River. The river had been named for the Indian tribes, and now the town was called Sioux Falls. A month later, representatives of the Dakota Land Company appeared. Finding the choicest site already occupied, they selected a second tract of 320 acres adjoining the first site, and named it Sioux Falls City.

---

* *Indians of the Dakotas*, p. 8

1858   A sacred white buffalo cow was killed by someone of the Swift Bear Band, noted for fast horses.

Commissioner Denver, echoing Thomas Jefferson, called for small reservations on which Indians would become farmers with their own land allotments.

1859   Pawnee potato diggers, discovered by the Sioux, were attacked and most of them killed.

1860   Sword winter. The government, for some unknown reason, issued swords to the chiefs.

1861   This year many babies and children died of an unknown disease.

Also, the Congress officially created Dakota Territory out of the plains that had once been Sioux hunting grounds. President Lincoln made the first territory appointments, choosing Dr. William Jayne of Springfield, Illinois for governor. Dr. Jayne set off for Yankton by horse and buggy.

1862   Death of Chief Turkey Leg.

The Minnesota Uprising this year alarmed Sioux throughout the West. The Santees had asked for new hunting grounds, as their old ones had been taken. Promised government supplies did not arrive, and they asked for food from a private store owner because they were hungry. The store owner, Nathan Myrick, said, "Let them eat grass." Following this and a long series of deceptions, the angered Santees went on a rampage, killing Myrick and other settlers, and taking many white hostages.

This was the year in which the Secretary of the Interior, Caleb Smith, proclaimed that Indians should be regarded as "wards of the government," no longer as independent nations. Here is the origin of the BIA's "trust powers" doctrine.

1863   In a battle with the Pawnees, the Sioux were badly defeated—nine of the bravest Sioux warriors were killed.

"The military confined its activities to garrisoning the military posts and keeping friendly and hostile Indians apart. . . .The military cordon included Fort Sully, established in 1863, at a site six miles below Fort Pierre."*

1864   This year nearly all the Sioux Bands camped together.

1865   The Omaha Dance was brought to the Sioux. The typical headdress of the Omahas was the roach.

A bill passed in Congress this year authorized new routes west through the great Teton buffalo ranges. Indian objections led to the council in Laramie. And Red Cloud, Oglala Sioux, led the Indian opposition to government proposals to construct forts along the Bozeman Trail to the Montana gold mines.

---

* Schell, pp. 84-5

"Red Cloud's War" brought victory to the Sioux and the Fort Laramie Treaty of 1868.

The Minneconjou band, on October 10, 1865, signed a treaty acknowledging the authority of the U. S.

1866   This winter was so severe that the cattle issued by the government were driven close to the tipis so the butchers could warm themselves often in the lodges.

On December 21, Captain William J. Fetterman led his eighty men into an ambush by the Sioux along the Bozeman Trail.

[Eighth Row]

1867   Chief Holy Bull met with the Great White Father in Washington. On his return the government issued two-wheeled, one-horse carts, the first wheeled vehicles the Sioux had.

1868   Blue Tipi winter. This year the government issued blue denim instead of white canvas.

"Under the Fort Laramie Treaty of 1868, the United States agreed to keep whites from hunting or settling on Indian territory; to abandon the proposed trail west; and to pay annuities for appropriated Indian lands. The treaty also established a Great Sioux Reservation which was to include all of what is now South Dakota west of the Missouri River. . . . The Indians were to release all lands east of the Missouri except for the. . .reservations previously created. By the end of 1868 nearly half of the Sioux were gathered onto reservations, and for two years, the conditions of the Fort Laramie Treaty were observed."*

1869   First Sioux child entered school. This was an Indian mission school established near Chamberlain, South Dakota.

As President Grant took office this year, his Peace Policy emerged, giving control of Indian agencies to Christian denominations rather than army officers, to further Indian education, to settle all tribes on reservations, etc. In effect, in spite of the reformers' optimism, this was essentially an assimilation policy to replace Jackson's policy of removal. Neither the Indians nor the frontier government ever thoroughly accepted it.

The U. S. Board of Indian Commissioners, whose members served without pay, to combat graft in the handling of Indian supplies and appropriations was commenced in this year. It continued until 1933.

1870   The winter the sun eclipsed.

During this winter, a Paiute shaman, named Tavibo, had a vision and prophesied to his Nevada tribe the end of the world and sure destruction of the hated white aggressors. The earth would be reborn and dead Indians would return to help the living ones establish an Indian paradise on earth. Using another eclipse of the sun (1888) and his foreknowledge of it from the white man's almanac, Tavibo's son, Wovoka, pointed to the great sign from the Heavens to stir his tribe into action. The frenzied Ghost Dance that developed and spread to the other tribes reached the Sioux Nation,

---

* *Indians of the Dakotas*, p. 9

and was later to trigger the Sioux Uprising of 1890.

But back in Dakota land in 1870, things were at a temporary calm. As a sign of good will between the red and the white man, Red Cloud with a large delegation of headmen and chiefs took a much publicized trip to Washington, D.C. and New York.

1871   Death of Chief Iron Whip.

On March 3, a rider attached to a Congressional appropriations bill abolished the practice of recognizing tribes as independent nations. This ended treaty making, and the requirement to abolish Indian title by treaty. Following this, official exchanges were made by executive order and acts of Congress.

In the same year, the Supreme Court in *McKay v. Campbell* held that Indians born in tribal allegiance are excluded from U. S. citizenship rights, because "Indian tribes. . . have always been held to be distinct and independent political communities, retaining the right of self-government. . ."

1872   Chief Black Bird visited the Oglalas to conduct the Corn Dance ceremony.

Surveyors for the Northern Pacific Railroad were harried by bands of Dakota.

1873   Standing Cloud kept a sacred white buffalo robe.

1874   One hundred Pawnees, including women and children, were killed in a battle by the Sioux along the Platte River.

Gold seekers were rushing into the Black Hills following an announcement by General George A. Custer that his men had found gold there. The government ordered the soldiers to keep the prospectors off the Indian land, but they could not. The Dakota were annoyed but patient.

1875   Chief Smoke Maker whipped an Omaha and released him unharmed. High-topped moccasins were typical of the Omahas.

In the fall, several Dakota bands left their reservations after getting government permission to hunt in the Powder River country.

Congress passed the Indian Homestead Act, granting Indian heads of families the same 160 acres of land as under the General Homestead Act of 1862, if they would give up their tribal ways.

[Ninth Row]

1876   The Omahas and the Sioux made a treaty of everlasting peace.

It is interesting to note that no recognition of the Battle of the Little Big Horn was made by the historian of the Big Missouri Winter Count. In January of this year the Dakota who had been hunting in the Powder River country were ordered to return immediately to the reservation. The Indians, with practically no food and in extremely cold weather, could not travel, so remained where they were. As a result General George Crook was ordered to attack the camp of Crazy Horse the following summer. Oglala Dakota Crazy Horse and Sitting Bull of the Hunkpapas led the warriors who annihilated Custer and his 224 soldiers.

In the following fall, the Black Hills were appropriated by Congress, violating the 1868 treaty; and the Deadwood stage made its first run.

1877   The first government issue station for the Lower Brulés is established at what is now Oacoma.

Chief Crazy Horse is killed. White Cow Killer in his winter count calls it "Crazy-Horse-killed-winter." American Horse drew a picture of an Indian, with the scalp lock that distinguished the Dakota, with a bayonet stuck in his groin and above him a horse's head with a wavy line (indicating crazy) from the horse to the man's head. Winter counts were necessarily local in nature, and the group of Tetons along the Missouri apparently were not primarily concerned with the history-making events going on to the west of the Black Hills.

Apart from Sitting Bull's resistance in the North and the conflicts of 1890, military warfare against the U. S. government was virtually over.

February 28, 1877 marks the establishment in Congress of the Standing Rock Reservation for the Blackfoot, Hunkpapa, Lower and Upper Yanktonais Sioux.

1878   Four-wheeled wagons were issued this year for the first time.

Cattlemen were entering the range lands of southern Dakota Territory. Miners had claimed the sacred Black Hills of the Indian. White Cow Killer calls it "Wagons given to the Dakota Indians Winter."

A Congressional appropriation established an Indian police force at all agencies.

1879   Rosebud Indian Agency established.

The Carlisle Indian School was founded in Pennsylvania for the U. S. government by Captain R. H. Pratt. His policy—"to civilize the Indian, put him in the midst of civilization. To keep him civilized, keep him there."

1880   A great Sun Dance was held at Blackpipe, now Norris, South Dakota.

"The summit of Sioux religious expression was the Sun Dance, an annual ritual performed during the summer encampment and lasting several days. Among the Teton Sioux, and some other Plains tribes, the Sun Dance was climaxed by a form of self-torture in which the dancers attempted to pull free from a skewer which pierced their breast muscles. . . . The skewer was secured by a rope attached to a central pole 20 or 30 feet from the dancer. This performance was a demonstration of the dancer's physical endurance and represented the most powerful of all varieties of Sun Dance vows."* The government later outlawed the dance and forbad any Sioux to take part in a Sun Dance festival.

1881   Blizzards were so severe nearly all horses were frozen.

Most of the Dakota bands that had escaped to Canada under Sitting Bull, following the defeat of Custer, returned to the United States under Gall, surrendered and were taken to the Standing Rock Reservation.

---

* *Indians of the Dakotas*, p. 7

1882   Chief Spotted Tail killed by Crow Dog.

"The case of Crow Dog, who had murdered Chief Spotted Tail near the Brulé Agency at Rosebud in August 1881, had focused national attention on the anomaly of employing tribal law for expiating Indian crime. Crow Dog had submitted to arrest and was sentenced to hang following his conviction in 1882 in a Deadwood district court. The Supreme Court of the United States held, however, that the Dakota courts lacked jurisdiction and that, moreover, Crow Dog had made sufficient atonement to the victim's family by paying blood money in the form of ponies. The Crow Dog case, and similar incidents at Rosebud and other agencies prompted the decision to set up Indian courts and to extend the jurisdiction of the United States Government to major offenses."[*]

As part of the "Dakota Boom," Congress ceded half of the Sioux Reservation to settlement for cash.

1883   Dog Shield died. His grieving wife hung herself and they were buried together.

1884   Egg on the Head, brutal and insolent, was killed by a white woodchopper near the mouth of Whetstone Creek.

---

[*] Schell, p. 319

[Tenth Row]

1885   Chief White Thunder was killed by the son of Spotted Tail.

In this year, an act of Congress established federal jurisdiction over major criminal offenses in Indian Territory.

By this year, the buffalo were virtually gone from the northern plains. 1880 had marked their disappearance from the southern plains.

1886   Chief Little Prairie Chicken, refusing to accept an allotment of land, was imprisoned.

1887   The Winter of the Night Issue. The Sioux, enraged by the government's refusal to issue clothing until allotments of land had been accepted, threw Major Spencer, Agent, from his office. Demanding the warehouse keys from yard boss, Helzer, the chiefs entered and issued the clothing at night.

In the General Allotment Act, Congress radically changed Indian affairs by establishing general individual Indian ownership of land. Citizenship followed ownership, under its provisions, as did more control by local agents. The "surplus" after allotment was open for settlement, reducing Indian land from 140 million to 50 million acres.

This also was the year in which the Commissioner prohibited use of Indian languages in Indian schools.

1888   The winter when the stomachs of two women were tapped. An unknown ailment effecting [sic] two women caused great bloating. The agency physician tapped their stomachs, but both women died.

Congress enacted a law providing that any Indian woman could gain citizenship by marriage to a U. S. citizen.

1889   Willard J. Cleveland, an Episcopal missionary known as "Long Pine," came to counsel with the Sioux on the acceptance of land allotments.

North Dakota, South Dakota, Montana and Washington became states.

1890   General Crook, known as "Three Stars," made a treaty for the Sioux to accept land allotments.

In October, Kicking Bear brought the Ghost Dance to Sitting Bull's camp. The new religion spread like wildfire in the Hunkpapa camp where the Indians were eager to talk with their dead and to restore control of their hunting grounds. On December 29, 3000 troops were called in "to maintain peace" in Dakota country. This was climaxed by the Wounded Knee Massacre. This tragedy ended for all time armed opposition from the Indians, and from then on their history is bound up with "government issue."

1891   End of the Ghost Dance. Big Foot, of Standing Rock and one of the leaders of Short Bull's Ghost Dance, wore feathers on his wrist and in his hair. His shirt was said to be impervious to whiteman's bullets. When soldiers attempted to capture Big Foot and his camp, Sitting Bull was killed with several comrades.

Big Foot was later killed in the massacre at Wounded Knee.

1892   The winter two head of cattle were issued to every man, woman and child.

The reputations earned by corrupt Indian agents during the 1860's and 1870's continued to plague their successors at the Dakota agencies long after the introduction of higher standards of conduct were insisted upon and agents chosen for merit. This improvement was the result of an investigation by Theodore Roosevelt in 1892.

1893   Death of the medicine man, Iron Sided Bear.

[Eleventh Row]

1894   The Sioux received the first per capita payment from the government. Each man, woman and child received $30.

1895   Holy Bull and other Lower Brulé Sioux tried to establish their homes on the Rosebud Reservation near Hamill, South Dakota, while Crooked Foot, another Lower Brulé, was bound and dragged to the Lower Brulé Reservation where the police held all the Lower Brulé people for two years.

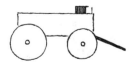

1896   The government divided Lower Brulé Reservation into allotments and issued regular Sioux benefits including wagons.

1897   Some Lower Brulé Sioux made an agreement with the Rosebud Sioux, approved by the Government, to return to the Rosebud Reservation and settle along the Big White River near Hamill, South Dakota.

1898   A Washington official made final agreement for the adoption of certain Lower Brulé Sioux by the Rosebud Sioux. This was the second time the Sioux were required to "touch the pen" in signing an agreement.

1899   Swimmer, respected Sioux policeman, broke his leg. While on official duty, his horse fell on him and the break was so serious, the leg was amputated.

In *Stephens v. Cherokee Nation*, the U. S. Supreme Court maintained that Congress holds "plenary power of legislation" over Indian tribes.

1900   The government built a commissary at Hamill, South Dakota, for the adopted Lower Brulé Sioux.

1901   The Winter Bad Dog died—the only person who caught smallpox that year.

1902   *Sioux agreed to the opening and settlement of Gregory County, South Dakota.*

The U. S. Supreme Court ruled, in *Lone Wolf v. Hitchcock,* that Congress may decide whether past treaty provisions are in the interests of the U. S. and the Indians, and may waive those provisions when they so choose.

[Twelfth Row]

1903   *The Winter Walking Shield and George Bear were hung. Walking Shield killed an old woman in order to elope with her daughter. George Bear killed a half-breed named John Shaw and later the same day killed a school teacher at the Milks Camp Day School. Both were hanged together at Sioux Falls.*

1904   *Some Pine Ridge Sioux went hunting in Wyoming and got into trouble with officers of that state.*

The eastern end of the Rosebud Reservation was opened for settlement by Presidential proclamation, followed by similar measures in 1907 and 1910, and on the Pine Ridge Reservation.

1905   *The wife of Leader Charge gave birth to quadruplets.*

1906   *Edwin Jordan, son of Col. Charles P. Jordan, a trader at Rosebud Agency, drowned while riding across a dam on horseback.*

1907   *Death of Chief White Blanket.*

1908   *Sitting Eagle, a noted Indian policeman, committed suicide.*

The Milwaukee railroad which cut through Dakota land had now been completed across Montana. The "Iron Horse" had replaced the Indian pony on the Plains.

1909   *Death of Chief Swift Bear, famous for his swift horses.*

1910   *The government issued silver dollars at night. Since the districts were so far apart, nightfall arrived before the issue was completed.*

Homesteaders were taking up land in Dakota and Montana.

1911   *Death of Eagle Bear.*

[Thirteenth Row]

1912   *Turning Bear, a prominent man, was killed by a passenger train at Valentine, Nebraska.*

1913   Death of Chief Hollow Horn Bear, famed for his oratory and leadership, in Washington, D.C. where he was taking part in the inauguration ceremony.

1914   Death of Chief Two Strike, a noted warrior.

1915   Death of Chief High Bear.

1916   George Pony and his wife were killed by their cruel son-in-law, James Fisherman, a Cheyenne River Sioux, because they refused to return their daughter to him. Fisherman was sentenced to life in the State Penitentiary.

The U. S. Supreme Court, in this year, ruled in *U. S. v. Nice* that Congress may direct the affairs of any Indian who has become a citizen (by Congressional act), and may still consider that Indian a ward of the government.

1917   Death of Chief Whirlwind Soldier.

1918   Many young men joined the Army to fight in World War I.

[Fourteenth Row]

1919   Two girls deserted St. Francis School on a very cold day. One girl froze to death, the other's feet were so frozen they had to be amputated.

As early as 1870, the government had set up a day school on the Yankton Reservation, but early provision for Indian education was left mainly in the hands of the missionaries. Later the government maintained day schools, reservation boarding schools, and non-reservation boarding schools.

Congress passed an act on November 6, granting citizenship to Indian men enlisting in military service.

1920   Death of Big Turkey.

1921   Two boys deserted St. Francis School on a very cold day. One boy froze to death, the other survived.

1922   Commissioner of Indian Affairs Burke visited Rosebud and gave good advice.

1923   Eagle Elk, a prominent medicine man, was arrested by agency officials while conducting a ceremony.

In this year, the American Indian Defense Association was founded to preserve tribal cultures.

1924   A buffalo feast honoring Ralph H. Case, attorney for the Sioux, was held. The buffalo came from the preserve near Valentine, Nebraska.

In 1924, all Indians were declared citizens!

1925   Wheeler Bridge completed. This was the first bridge across the Missouri River connecting Rosebud country with the East.

1926   James H. McGregor, a good agent, left.

The Interpretation ends with the figure of McGregor waving his hat in farewell. There is one more figure on the buffalo hide. The hair and lack of hat would indicate an Indian; the black clothes would indicate a missionary. Perhaps it is Kills Two's signature to mark the end of a pictured record and a troubled, tragic era for the Sioux. One hundred and thirty-one winters had been counted; the carefully preserved skin was filled; and the Indian had lost his valiant battle for the Big Missouri valley and the West. The Dakota historians had preserved the story for all men to see.

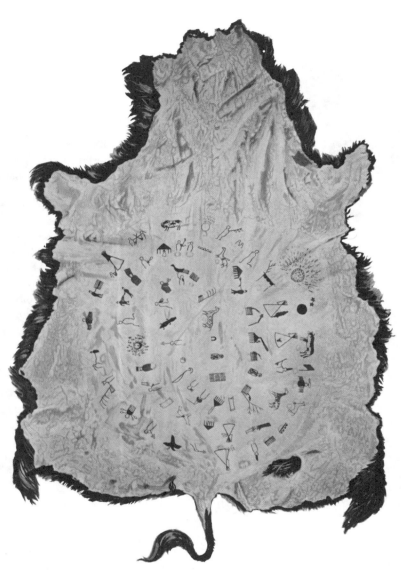

The Lone Dog Winter Count traces the years 1801 to 1871 along a counterclockwise spiral outward from the center.

II

ADDITIONAL WINTER COUNTS

The first winter count to be brought to the attention of white historians was that calendar kept by Lone Dog from 1801 to 1871 (Illustration on page 50). Copies of it were obtained and an interpretation was compiled through conversations with many Indians at Fort Sully and Fort Rice, Dakota Territory, in 1876. A scholarly paper entitled "A Calendar of the Dakota Nation" was issued in April 1877 in *Bulletin No. 1* of the United States Geological and Geographical Survey, and was later published in the 1882-83 *Annual Report* of the Bureau of American Ethnology of the Smithsonian Institution.*

The original pictures were drawn upon a buffalo skin, but the Indian historian allowed copies of it to be made on cotton cloth for Lt. H. T. Reed, First U. S. Infantry, who was then instrumental in getting explanations of the chart from knowledgeable Indians.

Lone Dog, in 1876, was an aged Indian belonging to the Yanktonai tribe of the Dakota Nation. At this time Lone Dog was living at Fort Peck, Montana Territory, and is believed to have still had in his possession the original skin upon which winters had been marked for almost three-quarters of a century. Although Lone Dog was a very old man, it was not supposed that he was of sufficient age in the year 1800 to begin the record. Either there was a predecessor who had kept the chart, or at the time he had begun to keep the record he had gathered the information from elders and worked back as far as he could do so accurately.

Most Indians interviewed by the writer of the 1877 paper had some knowledge of Lone Dog's Count. This is thought to have been a record for the whole Dakota Nation, rather than for any specific tribe, and many copies of it were made by members for more ready access to its information. Shortly after 1877, other winter counts were discovered within the Dakota Nation. Dr. William Corbusier, Assistant

---

* Powell.

Surgeon with the United States Army, collected several. The most complete ones were those credited to Baptiste (Battiste) Good, American Horse, Cloud Shield, and White Cow Killer.

Two other counts that are similar to Lone Dog's are the ones kept by The Swan and by The Flame (sometimes called The Blaze). These three counts are reproduced for purposes of comparison in the 1882-83 *Report* of the Bureau of Ethnology in three parallel columns. Though the drawings differ, it is obvious that the subject matter is the same in almost all cases. An epidemic of smallpox, a famine, an eclipse of the moon, or the coming of a missionary are events that are consistently noted and can be dated according to the whiteman's calendar.

A comparison of the Big Missouri Winter Count to those in the Smithsonian records reveals very little similarity of events. The all-encompassing things such as smallpox epidemics, moon eclipses and hard winters are noted on all of them. But the local events recorded by the Big Missouri historian are entirely different and indicate that this count was not a copy of Lone Dog's work.

In 1962 a bulletin entitled *The Sioux, 1798-1922, A Dakota Winter Count,* by Alexis Praus, was published by the Cranbrook Institute of Science. It describes a winter count, now known as the Cranbrook Count, which is a series of pictures drawn upon a heavy duck cloth of the kind once issued to the Indians by the government as a substitute for animal skins in making tipis. The cloth measures 34 by 35½ inches, and it is assumed by the writer of the bulletin that the count now in possession of the Cranbrook Institute is a copy of one originally drawn on a cured animal skin. The drawings "are arranged in spiral form, from the outer edge of the cloth toward the center. Starting in the upper left hand corner, 125 pictographs of varying size are encompassed by free-drawn lines forming rectangles of unequal dimensions." This count covers a span of 125 years, and its interpretation has been researched and reported by Mr. Praus.

Red Horse Owner's Winter Count, edited by Joseph S. Karol from information supplied by the granddaughters of Moses Red Horse Owner, was published in 1969. This count is unique in that it has been kept up to date (1786 to 1968) by these girls, Angelique Fire Thunder and Lydia Fire Thunder Bluebird. It is unique also in that the interpretation for each pictograph is written beside it in the Dakota language. "Moses had been ailing with gall stones, and as he lay in his bed, he liked to draw and decided to make the Winter Count book, in which he drew pictures dating from 1786," wrote Angelique Fire Thunder in her biography of the grandfather who could read in Dakota, had read the Dakota Bible through, and had memorized the complete Dakota version of the Episcopal Prayer Book.

After Moses Red Horse Owner's death, Angelique learned the meaning of each pictograph from her grandmother, Louisa. The young girl transferred each pictograph to a notebook wherein she also wrote out the interpretation in the Dakota language with the help of Louisa. English translations are also given as a part of the text in the book. Lydia, to whom the book was given in 1926, asked Butch Stoldt to draw the pictures on a tanned goat skin, and this was done in 1935.

Similar counts were kept by the Cheyenne, and other tribes, but the present book deals only with those known to have been kept by the Dakota Nation.

The pictographic records, preserved and understood by members of the tribe, could be used and referred to with sufficient ease and accuracy for ordinary purposes. Definite signs for the first capture of wild horses and the first appearance of smallpox among the Dakota were dates as satisfactory from which to count time as the white man's A.D. 1802 and 1813 were to him.

The careful arrangement of distinctly separate characters in rows across the buffalo skin or in an outward spiral starting from the center is an ingenious expedient to dispense with the use of numbers for noting years, yet allows every date to be determined by counting backward and forward from any other that might be known.

III

WINTER COUNT PATTERNS

As mentioned in the Introduction, the Big Missouri Winter Count, shown in the front of this text, reads as does a book, from left to right, and from top to bottom. The hoof marks in the upper left corner mark the beginning of this record. Next to them is a braceleted hand to indicate the death of Chief Bone Bracelet, and one reads on to the death of Chief Buffalo Tail on the Head. The first line ends with the picture of a pregnant woman to record that the very cold winter took the lives of many expectant mothers. From there one goes to line two which pictures the arrival of two "friendly white women."

The Lone Dog Winter Count (Illustration on page 50) begins in the center of the skin with a series of short straight lines bordered with long black lines to indicate the death of thirty-one Dakota killed by the Crows. Reading right to left one finds that the next figure represents a person covered with red spots to record a devastating smallpox epidemic. The hoof mark has now become a horseshoe to indicate the first horses that Indians had seen wearing metal shoes. A curly-tufted horse is next, then a long-stemmed pipe decorated with streamers, signifying a war dance; again the short lines bordered by long ones record eight Dakota killed by Crows. The eagle figure starts the reader around the circular pattern which records the 71 years following 1800.

An entirely different pattern appears in the chart kept by Bodie, called The Flame, or The Blaze. His record, which begins in 1786 and runs through 1876, begins at the lower left-hand corner of the skin and proceeds in a straight line to the right, then, moving up one line, proceeds toward the left. When the left extremity of the skin has been reached the artist moves up another line and goes from left to right again, making a serpentine pattern to the top of the hide. This pattern of writing was known to ancient Greeks, and the technical word for it, "boustrophedon," means, literally, turning as an oxen does in plowing.

A Minneconjou Dakota chief, known as The Swan, or The Little Swan, chose a spiral pattern similar to that of Lone Dog for his calendar, but the figures form an oval rather than a circle, and they read from left to right.

An elongated spiral two feet, six inches, by one foot, six inches, was devised by Mato Sapa, called Black Bear. This Minneconjou warrior drew one pictograph for each year, and worked from right to left.

Red Horse Owner's Winter Count follows the pattern of lines proceeding from left to right, as in a book. Moses Red Horse Owner drew the pictographs originally as he recalled events of the years past. Later they were copied into a lined school notebook by his granddaughter, who also supplied the interpretations in the Dakota language. When the pictures were copied on a tanned goat skin by Butch Stoldt, he also followed the left-to-right and top-to-bottom pattern.

There seems to have been no uniformity of design, but each historian chose a pattern that had continuity and was easy to follow. Years could be counted backward or forward from any picture with equal accuracy and ease. Though it seems evident that some of these winter count records were copied from one original (possibly Lone Dog's), the new recorder reproduced the basic figures for each year, but he did not necessarily follow the design. The originality and the artistry of the American Indian are preserved in his winter counts.

IV

PICTOGRAPHS

Pictographs similar to those used in the winter counts were also found in carvings on rocks (petroglyphs) to record historical events and to list the members of a particular band of Indians. The name symbols were also put on drawings to indicate the artist and the subject.

Indian names given to children by parents or relatives were often changed as exploits or events gave rise to more significant names. This was more true with boys than with girls. The names often referred to some animal and predicated an attribute or position of that animal. Unusual physical characteristics of an individual sometimes gave rise to a name.

Since most of these names were objective, they could be illustrated in sign language and drawn in pictographs. Red and black were most often used, but some records also contain blue and yellow markings. A line drawn from the head of a man to a graphic picture above indicated that that was his name. Some Dakotas drew a line from the mouth of the character to the picture above to indicate the name relationship. An artist who drew a picture of himself signed his work by drawing his name picture and connecting it with a line to his head. The top illustration on page 57, as drawn by Sitting Bull, describes the action as he kills his enemies, and identifies himself as a warrior as well as the artist by the figure of a "sitting bull." Lean Wolf, a chief of the Hidatsas, represents himself, in the lower illustration on page 57, as a war chief by the horns on his bonnet and the upraised pipe in his hand. His name is shown by the figure of a wolf whose mouth is unfinished to indicate that there is nothing there, thus a lean wolf.

Pictographs were used by the Dakotas in submitting a roster of their clan members when they were required to do so by the government agents early in 1880. Chief Big Road of the Northern Oglalas brought in a list of 84 heads of families. Obviously done by the same artist, the outline of each head was much the same, but stripes across the cheek indicated rank, and a drawing above the head named each one. The illustrations on the top of page 58 show a representative few.

In the drawing above by Sitting Bull, a line from the horseman's mouth to the hoof of the "sitting bull" identifies the medicine warrior. (Photograph courtesy of the Smithsonian National Anthropological Archives, Bureau of American Ethnology Collection)

In the drawing below, Lean Wolf also represents himself wearing the horns of a war chief. He carries a pipe of leadership; and the symbol of his name floats behind, attached by a similar line. (Powell, p. 168)

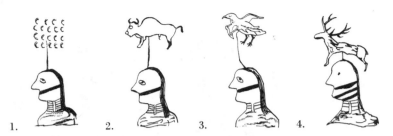

Heads of families in Chief Big Road's census of 1883 — 1. Brings Back Plenty 2. White Buffalo 3. The Real Hawk 4. Fast Elk

Red Cloud's census was taken in much the same way at the Pine Ridge Agency, but several artists worked on it. (See illustration below.) Some used only the pictograph to represent a name and did not draw the outline of a head for each man (or, in a few cases, woman) who was the leader of a family group. 289 members of Red Cloud's band were listed, and the English translations, or equivalent, of the names were written by an interpreter at the agency.

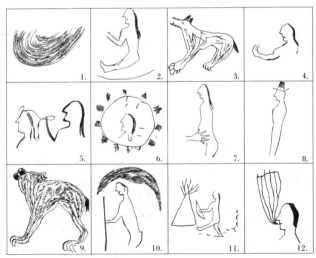

These pictographs represent a few of the 289 individuals in the 1880 census which was prepared under Red Cloud's supervision — 1. Red Cloud 2. Top Man 3. Slow Bear 4. Call For 5. Knock a Hole in the Head 6. Runs Around 7. Scratch the Belly 8. Tall White Man 9. Bear Looks Back 10. Old Cloud 11. Got There First 12. Big Voice

Red Cloud, himself, is depicted by semicircular lines. An arc with the open end upward always indicated sky, and in this case lines and shadings fill in the arc to portray a cloud. Top Man is shown as a man's figure above a sky arc, and Slow Bear is illustrated by a bear who is obviously holding back instead of running as animals are often drawn. Call For, as a name, is depicted by the sign language gesture of beckoning to someone. Knock a Hole in the Head required outline drawings of two men, one pounding a sharp object into the head of the other. Runs Around shows a man within a circle, and footsteps going around it. The lines within the circle indicate motion. Scratch the Belly was a name easy to depict. White men were always shown with hats, and the Indian named Tall White Man was easily represented by a few long lines with a head and hat.

A complete list of the individuals in Red Cloud's census and the drawings that depicted them are printed in the *Fourth Annual Report of the Bureau of American Ethnology of the Smithsonian Institution,* 1882-83.

V

THE DAKOTA NATION

Since Winter Counts are particularly associated with the Dakota (or Sioux) Nation, it might be well to look briefly at the groups that made up this great group of Plains Indians in the days when calendars were being drawn on buffalo skins.

Winter, by which they counted their years, was the longest season in that land along the Missouri River that stretches through eastern South Dakota and northern Nebraska (see map on page 62). It was also most impressive and respectful to say that a man was so many winters or snows old, or that so many snow seasons have passed since a certain event. Thus it was in keeping with the Indians' ideas that the year ended when the winter was over and new life began in the grass and the trees of the plains. It was a good time to think back over the year and to record it as history on the winter count skin.

The word Dakota is usually translated as meaning "leagued" or "allied." In the Dakota dialect, *cota* or *coda* means friend and may be literally translated to signify "our friends."

The word *Sioux* became a name bestowed on this Nation by white people, and it was indignantly repudiated by the Dakota people for many years. It has come into more common use in recent times. The members of the Nation have always preferred to be called Dakota. There is an unsavory connotation of the term *Sioux*. The Algonkin name for the Dakota was *Nadowessi*, according to the Bureau of Ethnology *Report*, and meant hated enemy or foe. The Ojibwas called them *Nadowessi*, meaning "little rattlesnake" or "viper." The French voyageurs picked up that name, gave it their own plural form, *Nadowessioux*, and then cut it down to *Sioux*.

The more important of the western division which existed during the years that winter counts were kept are listed in the Smithsonian report* as the following: Yankton and Yanktonai, Blackfoot, Two

---

* Powell.

Kettle, Without Bows (Sans Arcs), Minneconjou, Burnt Hip or Brulé, Oglala, and Hunkpapa or Unkpapa. Titon, from the word *titan* (and usually spelled Teton), meant "at or on land without trees." It was the name used to indicate that aggregation of tribes that left the eastern woodlands and moved onto the Plains in the West, including the tribes or bands mentioned above. Whites have confused the term with the French word *teton*, meaning "woman's breast," in allusion to the form of certain mountain peaks of the region.

These tribal divisions were believed to have come from The Seven Great Council Fires, known in tradition and encountered by the very early white explorers and settlers.

Much of the history of these people has been lost, but the preserved winter counts record a century of events that is roughly encompassed by the dates 1800 to 1900.

Throughout the ages, man has recorded his activities. The cave dweller carved or painted pictures on the rocks; the early Egyptians buried household equipment and tools with their dead; great artists in Europe preserved the concepts of their religion by murals in cathedrals and by marble statues. After the printing press was invented in the early 1400's, the European began recording history on printed pages bound into books.

The Dakota Indian recorded time and events with his winter count. The pictures, drawn upon a well-cured skin, illustrate two skills for which the first American is renowned: his ability to say much in very few words, and his talent for drawing and artistry. No words were used on the winter counts because the Dakota language was a spoken one, but the Indian artist made a small drawing tell a whole story.

The Big Missouri Winter Count tells the story of the people who lived along this big, always muddy river as they hunted buffalo, gave thanks for plenty, suffered through starvation and disease, fought their enemies, mourned their dead, and watched the white men come to their land.

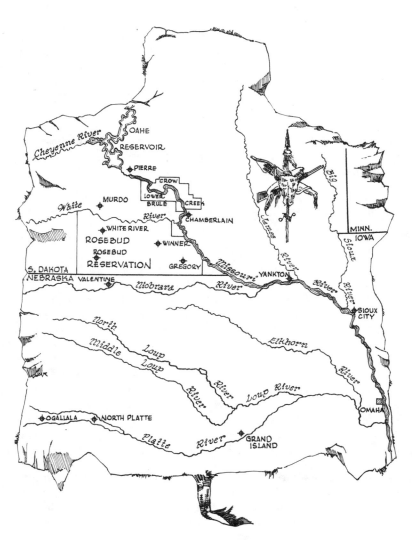

The muddy river country of the Big Missouri Winter Count

BIBLIOGRAPHY

ABC-CLIO Electronic Library. "Winter Count." *Bibliography of Native North Americans on Disc (1500–)*. Dataware Technologies, Inc., 1994.

Brotherston, Gordon, ed. "A Sioux Winter Count, 1800-70." In *Image of the New World; The American Continent Portrayed in Native Texts*. London: Thames and Hudson, 1979, pp. 131-32.

Bureau of Indian Affairs. U.S. Department of the Interior, *Famous Indians: A Collection of Short Biographies*. Washington, DC: Government Printing Office (no date).

Bureau of Indian Affairs, U.S. Dept. of the Interior. *Indians of the Dakotas*. Washington DC: Government Printing Office (no date).

"Calendar for Oglala Sioux Names for Years from A.D. 1759 to A.D. 1908." Three-page mimeographed list.

Chief Eagle, D. *Winter Count*. Denver: Golden Bell Press, 1968. Also Colorado Springs: Dentan-Berkeland, 1967.

Cohen, L.K. "Big Missouri's Winter Count—A Sioux Calendar 1796-1926." *Indians at Work* (1939) 6, no. 6: 16-20.

_____ "Swift Bear's Winter Count." *Indians at Work* (1942) 9, no. 6: 30-31 and (1942) 9, no. 7:29-30.

Dempsey, Hugh Aylmer. *A Blackfoot Winter Count*. Calgary: Alta, 1965; reprint Calgary: Glenbow Foundation, Alberta Institute, 1970.

Finster, David. *The Hardin Winter Count*. "News," 29:3/4. Vermillion, South Dakota, University of South Dakota Museum: 1968.

Glandy, Diane. *Lone Dog's Winter Count*. Albuquerque, New Mexico: West End Press, 1991.

Grange, Roger Tibbetts, Jr. "The Garnier Oglala Winter Count." *Plains Anthropologist* (1963) 8:744-79.

Higginbotham, N. A. "The Wind-Roan Bear Winter Count." *Plains Anthropologist* (1981) 26, no. 91:1-42.

Howard, James Henri, ed. "Butterfly's Mandan Winter Count: 1833-1876." *Ethnohistory* (1960) 7:28-43.

_____ "Two Dakota Winter Count Texts." *Plains Anthropologist* (1955) 5:13-20.

_____ "Two Teton Dakota Winter Count Texts." *North Dakota History* (1960) 27:67–79.

_____ "Yanktonai Ethnohistory and the John K. Bear Winter Count." *Plains Anthropologist* (1976) No. 3, Memoir 11, p.78.

Karol, Joseph S., ed. *Red Horse Owner's Winter Count: The Oqlala Sioux, 1786–1968.* Martin, South Dakota: The Booster Publishing Co., 1969.

Kills Two. "Interpretation of the Big Missouri Winter Count." Typed copy deposited with the Big Missouri Winter Count skin in the Sioux Indian Museum. Rapid City, South Dakota.

Lavender, David. *The Rockies.* New York: Harper and Row, 1968.

McCoy, Ronald Timothy-Arvad. *Winter Count: The Teton Chronicles to 1799.* In *Dissertation Abstracts International.* No. 44: 8, 2554A. University Microfilms no. 8328348.

Miller, David Humphreys. *Ghost Dance.* New York: Duell, Sloan and Pearce, 1959.

Powell, J. W., director. *Fourth Annual Report of the Bureau of American Ethnology, 1882–83.* Washington, DC: Smithsonian Institution, 1886.

Praus, Alexis. *The Sioux, 1798–1922, A Dakota Winter Count.* Bulletin no. 44. Bloomfield Hills, Michigan: Cranbrook Institute of Science Press, 1962.

Raczka, Paul. M. *Winter Count: A History of the Blackfoot People.* Oldman River Culture Center, c. 1979.

Salisbury, Albert and Jane. *Two Captains West.* Seattle: Superior Press, 1950.

Schell, Herbert S. *History of South Dakota.* Lincoln: University of Nebraska Press, 1961.

Sioux Indian Museum, Rapid City, South Dakota. Photographs and information from the curator.

Smith, Marian Wesley. "Mandan 'history' as reflected in Butterfly's Winter Count." *Ethnohistory* (1960) 7: 199–205.

Vandervelde, Marjorie. "Winter Count" in Beatrice Levin, *Art of the American Indian.* Montana Indian Publication Fund, c. 1973.